make your own STINGRAY MODELS

Before you begin

This book shows you how to make superb Stingray models using materials recycled from around the house. By following the instructions and using the logos from the back of the book you can create stunning models, tough enough to survive hours of play.

The things you will need include:

- household junk, such as old shampoo containers and fabric conditioner bottles (see 'What You Need' for each model – in many cases specific materials are suggested, however, suitable alternatives should still create successful models.)
- paints - experiment with powder paints. powder paint mixed with PVA glue. Humbrol enamel model paint. grey metal paint, car paint sprays. Check all containers for safety details and use spray paints in a well ventilated place or outdoors.
- glues - use glues suitable for plastics – for example, Locktite. **UHU,** Bostick. Copydex or PVA children's glue
- turps to clean all brushes. This should only be used by adults.
- cutting tools – craft knife, scissors and junior hacksaw. Cutting should be done by adults or under adult supervision.
- newspaper to protect tables and other surfaces.

Check the safety details on all products used and keep all potentially toxic substances in a safe place.

Above all, be careful and have fun!

Stand by for action!

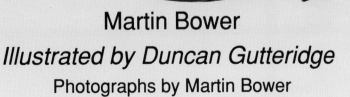

Martin Bower

Illustrated by Duncan Gutteridge

Photographs by Martin Bower

Hodder & Stoughton
LONDON SYDNEY AUCKLAND

STINGRAY

WHAT U NEED

* Large Vaseline Intensive Care bottle
* Cussons Aquaspa Hair & Body Wash bottle
* Clear, flat shampoo bottle
* Cutex nail varnish remover bottle
* Small 2 cm diameter bottle top
* Small clear plastic cup or bottle top approx 4 cm in diameter
* 3 small ballpoint pen tubes or mascara tubes
* 2 tiny dollshouse teaspoons
* UHU or Bostik glue
* Some stiff card or plastic sheeting
* Drill and junior hacksaw
* Plasticine or tape
* Silver, black, yellow, dark blue and mid-blue paint

To make the hull, cut the top off the Vaseline bottle and the screw section off the Cutex bottle. Remove the labels by soaking in water. Push the Cutex bottle inside the Vaseline bottle, as shown. Glue this in place with UHU or Bostik glue. You should have a small gap at each side which form the intakes.

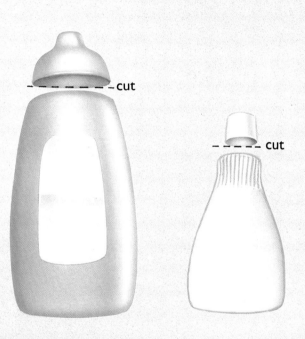

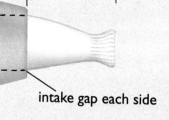

7.5 cm

intake gap each side

2

Cut the square lug and hook off the Aquaspa
bottle top. Stick the bottle top to the end of the
Vaseline bottle, as shown. This makes the front
of Stingray's hull. Fill in the little hole left where
the lug has been cut off with Plasticine, or cover
in with a piece of tape.

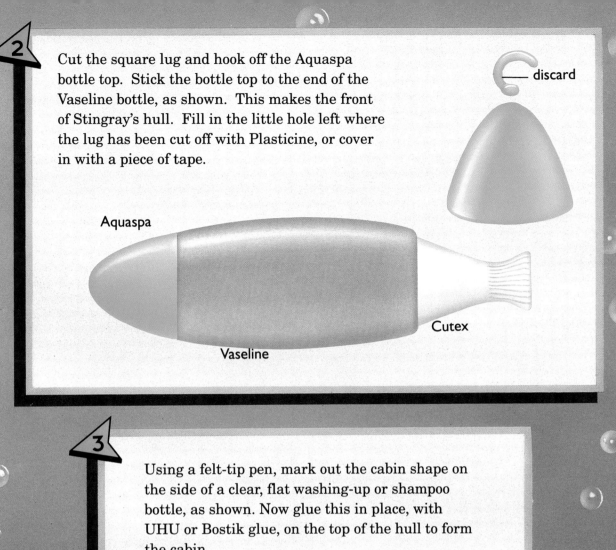

discard

Aquaspa

Vaseline

Cutex

3

Using a felt-tip pen, mark out the cabin shape on
the side of a clear, flat washing-up or shampoo
bottle, as shown. Now glue this in place, with
UHU or Bostik glue, on the top of the hull to form
the cabin.

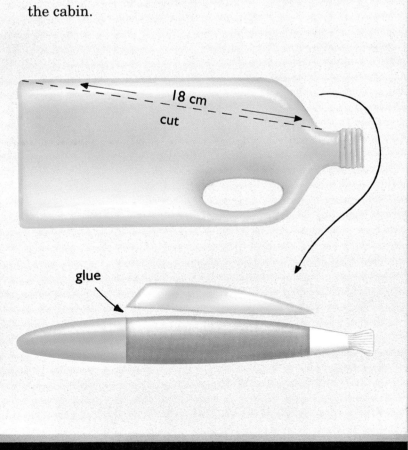

18 cm

cut

glue

4

Using the templates provided, mark out on stiff card, or plastic sheeting, two side fins, two dorsal fins and one tail fin. With a junior hacksaw, or craft knife, cut a slot up the sides of the Cutex bottle until the tail fin slides in, as shown. The cut-out for the rotor should come level with the end of the bottle, as shown.

slot along side

Next, glue the two dorsal fins to the back of the cabin, so that they stick out at angles as shown.

side fins (2)

fold

tail fin (1)

template

bottle

cut out

fold

dorsal fins (2)

5 Now stick the side fins in place, as shown. You can cut slots to fit them into if you want to make them stronger but this is not essential.

glue

glue

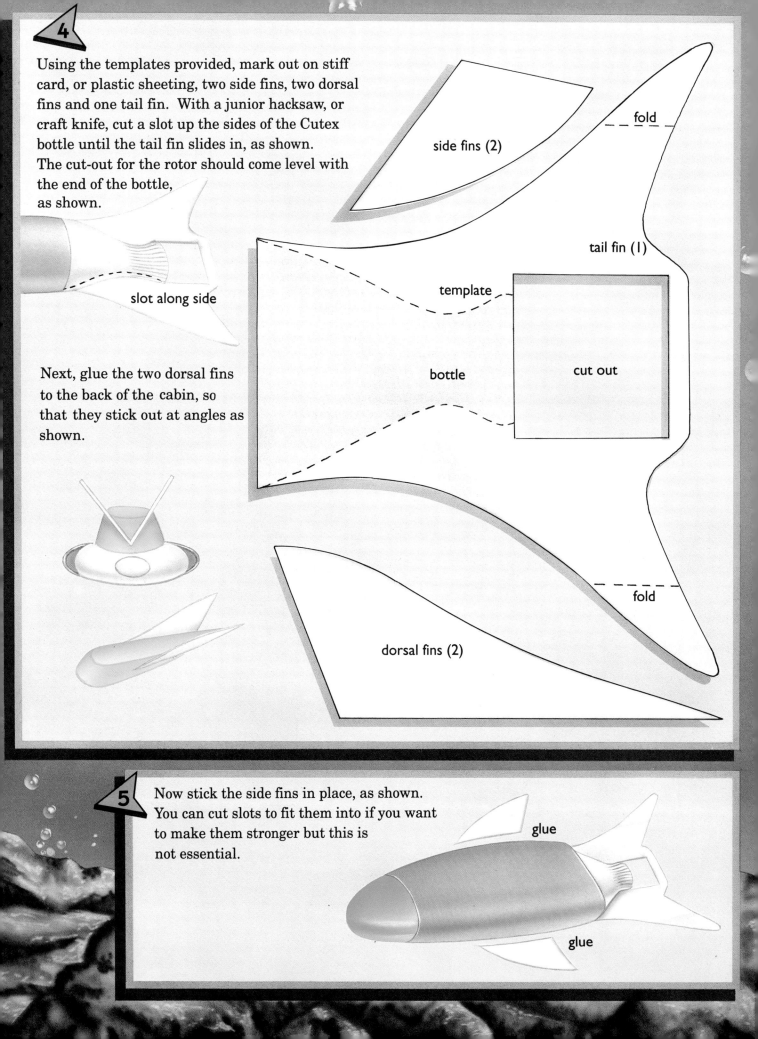

6

Take a bottle top with a diameter of not more than 2 cm and ask a grown-up to drill a hole at one edge large enough to take a pen tube, as shown. With a junior hacksaw cut both ends off the end of an old ballpoint pen tube or small mascara tube, as shown.

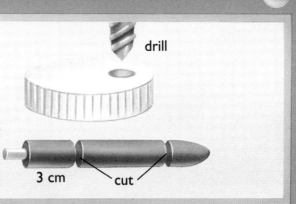

drill

3 cm   cut

7

Stick this in the hole you have drilled so that at least 2 cm sticks out. Now stick the pointed end of the same pen tube at right angles over the top of the tube to form the periscope. When this is done stick the whole assembly to the top of the cabin at the front, as shown.

push into hole and glue

discard

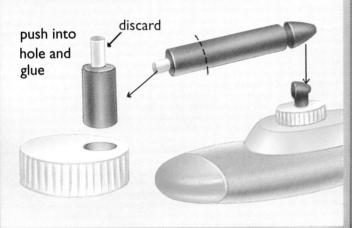

8

Remove the ends, nibs and ink tubes of the other two ballpoint pens. Discard these and cut the screw sections off the remaining tubes. Stick these under the side fins to form the aqua steering jets, as shown. You can use mascara tubes for these instead.

cut   discard

remove pen, nib and ink tube

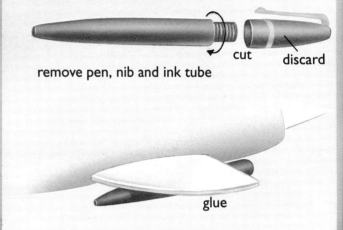

glue

9

Cut two strips of card or plastic sheeting, 1 cm wide and 12 cm long, and make them pointed at both ends, as shown. Stick these parallel to one another on the bottom of Stingray, in the position shown. These are the landing skids.

12 cm

1 cm

3 cm

7.5 cm

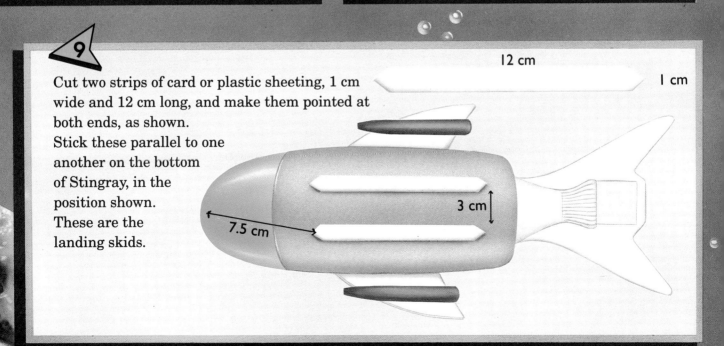

Now paint your model, using the photo as a guide. Use oil enamel paints (Humbrol) as these will stick to the plastic. Don't use water-based acrylic or poster paints. Start off by painting the whole model silver.

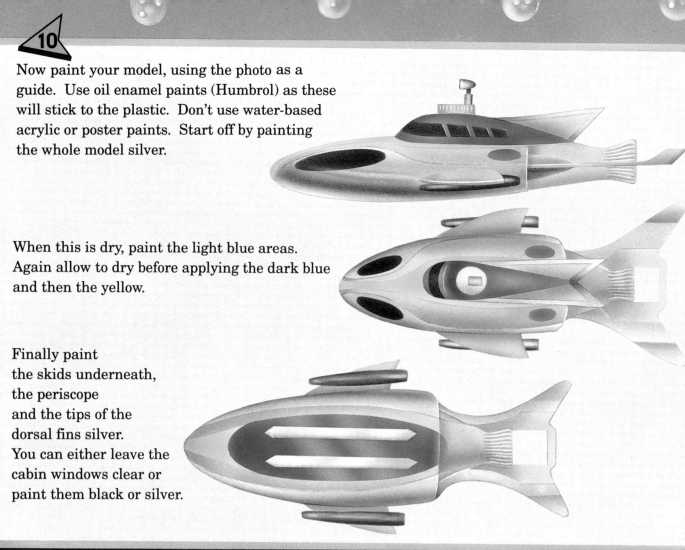

When this is dry, paint the light blue areas. Again allow to dry before applying the dark blue and then the yellow.

Finally paint the skids underneath, the periscope and the tips of the dorsal fins silver. You can either leave the cabin windows clear or paint them black or silver.

When all the paint is dry, stick the bowls of 2 dollshouse teaspoons onto each side, as shown, over the dark blue oval areas. These are the aquasprite canopies.

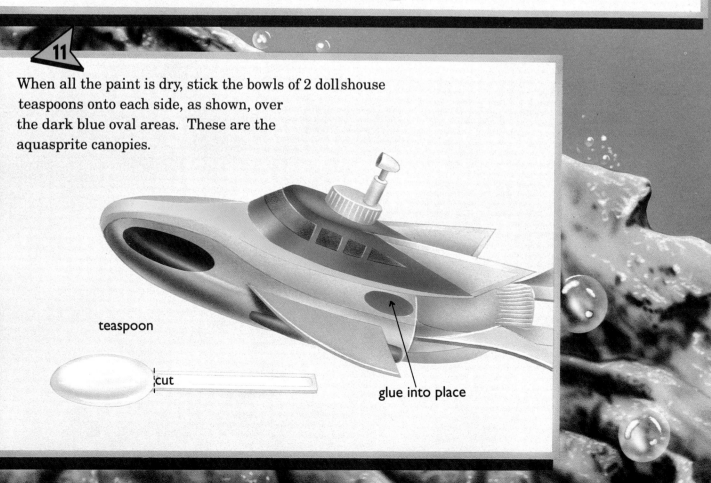

teaspoon

cut

glue into place

Finally cut the end off a clear plastic cup, as shown, to a length of 3.5 cm, or use a bottle top of the same size.(If you can find a clear top use this, but if   not paint it silver.) Lay the plastic cup,   or bottle top, onto a piece of card and draw   round it, as shown.

cut
3.5 cm

Cut this circle out and stick it to the open end of the cup or bottle top.

approx 4.5 cm

glue on

Stingray is ready for action!

Now stick this whole unit into the gap in the tail fin, as shown. To complete your model, cut out the Stingray logos from the back of the book and glue them into place.

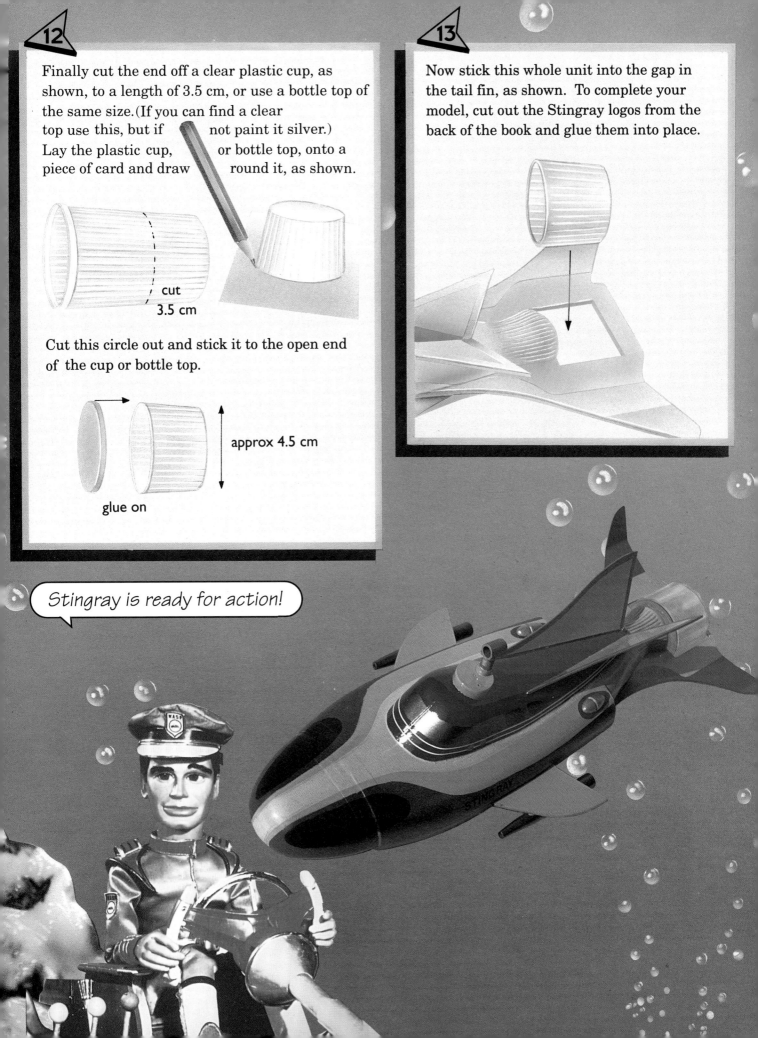

MARINEVILLE

* Large coffee jar lid
* Mazola cooking oil bottle
* 18 empty matchboxes
* 3 750 g cereal packets
* Grey cardboard eggbox
* 2 1 lb marmalade jar lids
* 2 200 g yoghurt tubs
* Packet of green railway modellers flock powder or sawdust
* UHU or Bostik glue
* A baseboard 50 cm x 40 cm (approx)
* Scissors, junior hacksaw and craft knife
* Pair of compasses
* Humbrol paints: brown, yellow, pale blue, red, grey, green

1

To make the control tower, cut the cooking oil bottle into three pieces, as shown. Keep the cap, top and bottom parts and discard the middle. Stick the cap and top onto the base of the bottle.

Then, stick the coffee jar lid over the open end of the bottle. You may need to trim the inside thread off the coffee lid with a sharp knife to make it fit properly, so get an adult to help you with this!

←discard

stick into recess →

2

Using the card from a cereal packet, cut three shapes to the size shown. Mark out all the dotted lines on the inside of the packet and, using a scissor blade, score along these dotted lines. Fold the shapes inwards to form cuboids and stick the edges together, tucking the gluing flaps inside.

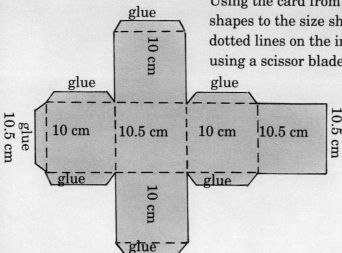

glue

10 cm

glue glue

glue
10.5 cm

10 cm | 10.5 cm | 10 cm | 10.5 cm

10.5 cm

glue glue

10 cm

glue

3

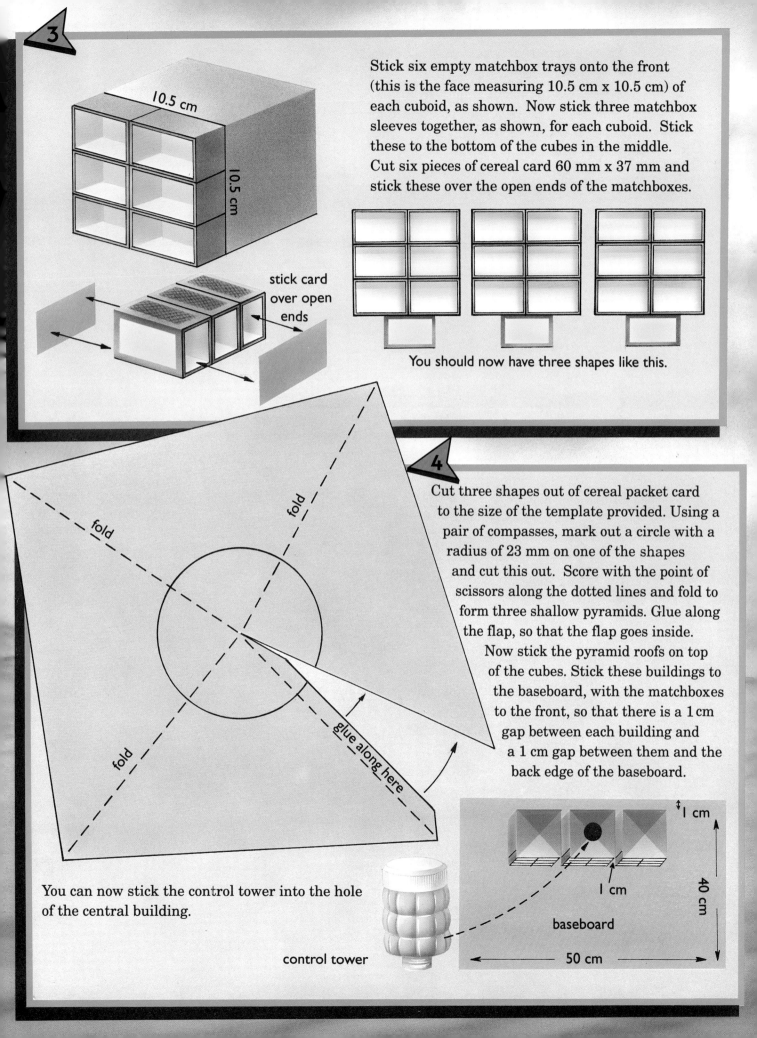

Stick six empty matchbox trays onto the front (this is the face measuring 10.5 cm x 10.5 cm) of each cuboid, as shown. Now stick three matchbox sleeves together, as shown, for each cuboid. Stick these to the bottom of the cubes in the middle. Cut six pieces of cereal card 60 mm x 37 mm and stick these over the open ends of the matchboxes.

10.5 cm

10.5 cm

stick card over open ends

You should now have three shapes like this.

4

Cut three shapes out of cereal packet card to the size of the template provided. Using a pair of compasses, mark out a circle with a radius of 23 mm on one of the shapes and cut this out. Score with the point of scissors along the dotted lines and fold to form three shallow pyramids. Glue along the flap, so that the flap goes inside.

Now stick the pyramid roofs on top of the cubes. Stick these buildings to the baseboard, with the matchboxes to the front, so that there is a 1 cm gap between each building and a 1 cm gap between them and the back edge of the baseboard.

fold

fold

fold

glue along here

You can now stick the control tower into the hole of the central building.

control tower

1 cm

1 cm

40 cm

baseboard

50 cm

5 Cut two struts from cereal packet card, following the template shown. Score and fold them to form a 'V' shape with the plain sides out. Stick these in position, as shown, so that they join the control tower with the roofs either side.

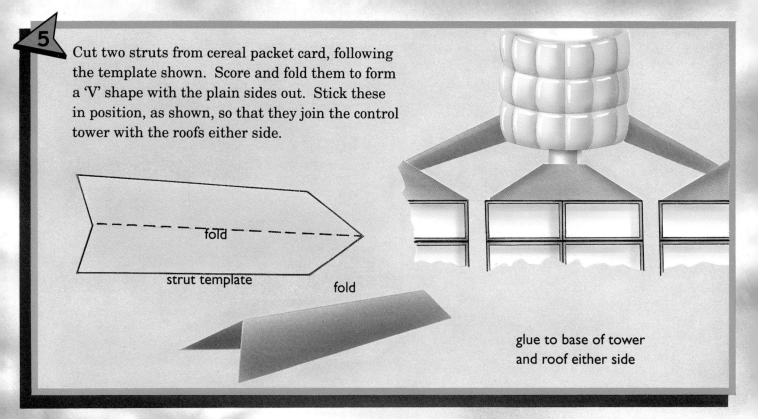

fold

strut template

fold

glue to base of tower and roof either side

6

Mark out the baseboard, as shown. Paint the roadway grey and allow to dry. Paint the grass area green and while the paint is still wet sprinkle the flock powder or sawdust onto it. When this is thoroughly dry brush off the excess. (If you use sawdust, you will need to paint it green after it has dried.)

Paint two 200 g yoghurt tubs silver and when they are dry, mark them out with a permanent marker as shown in the photo. Stick these in place on the grass.

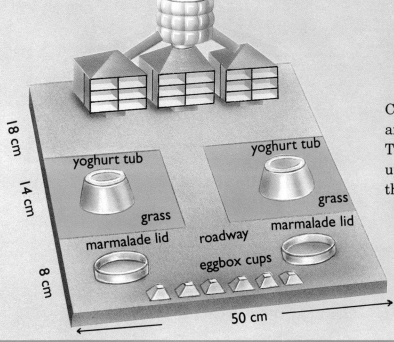

18 cm

14 cm

yoghurt tub

yoghurt tub

grass

grass

marmalade lid

roadway

marmalade lid

8 cm

eggbox cups

50 cm

Cut six cups from a cardboard eggbox and stick these where shown. Then stick two marmalade jar lids upside down where shown. These are the launch pads for the Interceptors!

7 Using the photo as a guide, paint Marineville with oil enamel (Humbrol) paints, in the colours shown. Use your imagination to decorate the model with other bits and pieces, such as lichen for bushes and plastic milk straws for pipes.

Mark out the roadway with ink marker and use white paint for the dotted lines.

Marineville is now ready for action because anything can happen in the next half hour!

X-2-ZERO'S CRAFT

WHAT U NEED

* Empty Radox shower/shampoo bottle
* Some cereal packet card or plastic sheeting
* 2 empty mascara or pen tubes
* Bottle top from Clairol hairspray
* Rubber stopper/washer and 1 toothpaste cap
* UHU or Bostik glue, sandpaper
* Henna shampoo bottle
* Junior hacksaw, craft knife
* Humbrol paint: silver, brown and red

1

Discard the Radox bottle top and, using a junior hacksaw or craft knife, cut the bottle, as shown. Smooth the edges with fine sandpaper or wet and dry paper. Stick the hairspray top tightly over the front of the bottle as far on as it will fit.

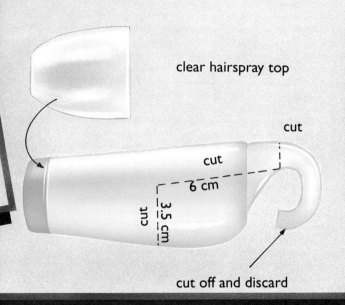

clear hairspray top

cut

cut

6 cm

3.5 cm

cut

cut off and discard

2

Cut two pieces of card to fit over the open ends of the bottle and glue in place, as shown.

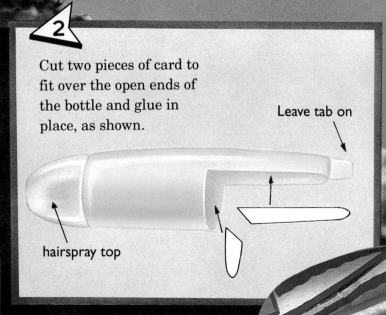

Leave tab on

hairspray top

3

Cut two tail fins, using the template for a guide, and stick these together, gluing round the edges only. Leave the front edge unglued, as shown. When the glue is dry, push the tail fin over the tab left on the end of the bottle, and stick in place.

Next cut a dorsal fin shape out of double thickness card and glue this in place where shown, 9.5 cm from the tail. Glue the toothpaste cap on the back, where shown, and the rubber stopper/washer on the nose.

dorsal fin →

9.5 cm

rubber stopper

toothpaste cap

tail fin

dorsal fin

do not glue this area

glue

glue

glue

glue

tail fin

4

Glue two empty mascara, or pen tubes, to the sides of the model, as shown. Finally, cut the top side off a Henna shampoo bottle, or similar, with a junior hacksaw. Smooth down the edges, with fine sandpaper or wet and dry paper, and glue this in place on the top of the craft, as shown, to form the cockpit/cabin section.

cut

glue in position

empty mascara or pen tubes

5

Paint X–2–Zero's craft with oil enamel paint, using the photo as a guide.

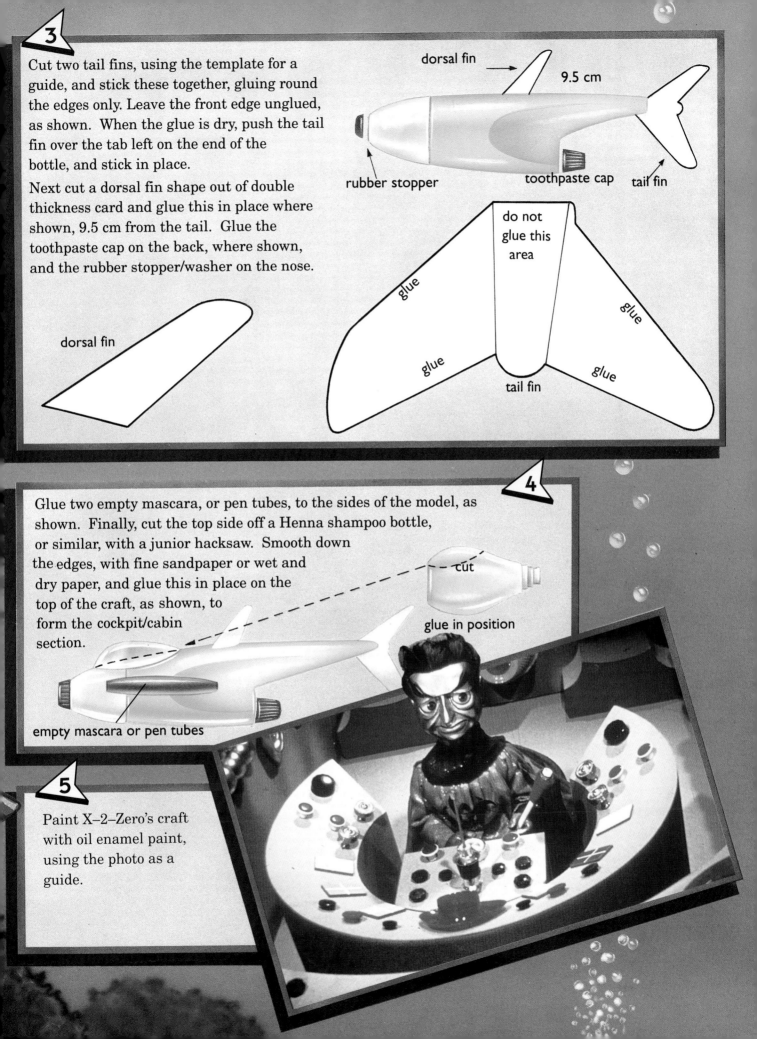

WASP ROCKET

WHAT U NEED

* 150 ml styling mousse container
* 2 styling mousse plastic tops
* Cutex lipstick top
* Cap from a litre can of engine-oil, or similar
* Bottle top
* Deodorant spray top
* Some cereal packet card
* UHU or Bostik glue
* Red, blue and silver enamel paint

1

Rough up the base of the mousse container and the top of the engine oil cap with sandpaper and glue them together, as shown.

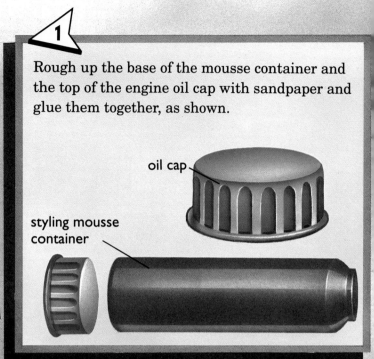

oil cap

styling mousse container

2

Rough up the top of the deodorant cap and glue this to the base of the oil cap.

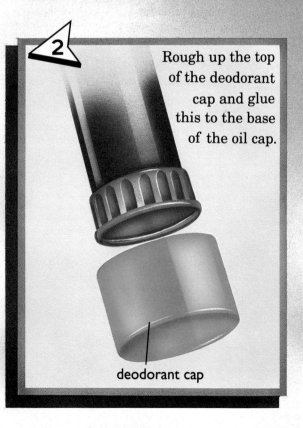

deodorant cap

3

Glue together the lipstick top, the bottle cap and the two styling mousse tops, as shown. Rough up all the surfaces before gluing.

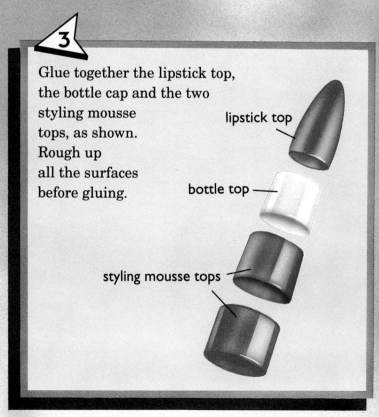

lipstick top

bottle top

styling mousse tops

4 Glue all sections together, as shown, to make the main rocket fuselage.

5 Using the two templates as guides, cut four small fins and four large fins out of double thickness cereal packet card, then glue them in place, where shown, at right angles to one another.

small fin template

large fin template

6 Paint the model with oil enamel paints, using the photo as a guide. Cut out the W.A.S.P. sticker and the chequered band from the back of the book and glue in place when the paint is dry.

You could make two of these models and stand them on the launch pads of your Marineville model!

TITANICA

1

Cut the fluid bottle into three pieces, as shown. Cut off the top and discard.

cut   cut

Stick one eggcup to the base of this bottle and the other eggcup to the base of a yoghurt tub.

yoghurt tub

WHAT U NEED

* 4 ping-pong balls
* 2 bottle tops
* Empty yoghurt tub and 4 empty yoghurt pots
* 2 cereal packets
* Zinc and castor-oil cream tub, or similar
* Empty Bar-B-Q lighting fluid bottle or white spirit bottle
* 2 shallow-tray eggcups
* 3 empty 1.2 KG washing powder cartons, or similar
* 2 empty cheese triangle boxes and one round margarine tub lid
* Large packet Polyfilla
* Some lichen from a model shop or some moss foliage
* A baseboard 60 cm x 50 cm
* 3 hand-cream lotion tops and 3 rubber washers
* Air-freshener top
* Junior hacksaw, craft knife, scissors
* 4 felt- tip pen tops
* UHU or Bostik glue
* Old table knife, stiff paint brush

2

Stick three hand-cream lotion tops to the top of the bottle and three rubber washers the sides of the yoghurt tub.

hand-cream tops

washers

3

Stick the top part of the bottle onto the lid of a margarine tub and then stick this onto the air- freshener top.

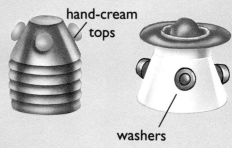

— margarine lid

— air-freshener

You now have buildings 1, 2 and 3.

Cut a circle with a diameter of 12 cm out of cereal packet card. Cut another circle with a diameter of 13 cm also out of card. Draw a line from the edge of the large circle to the centre point and cut along this. Now overlap one edge over the other to form a shallow cone measuring 12 cm in diameter, then glue the overlapped edges together. Glue this cone to the smaller disc or card. This is the roof.

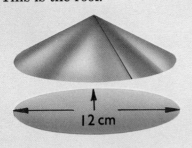

12 cm

Cut a strip of card, 3 cm wide and 30 cm long, with a serrated edge, and glue this around the edge of the zinc and castor oil cream tub.

Glue the roof over the open end of the tub.

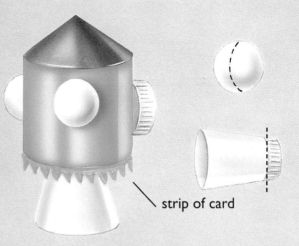

strip of card

Then cut the base from a yoghurt pot and cut this to fit the side of the tub. Glue in place. Cut two ping-pong balls in half and glue to tub, as shown. Finally, stick the whole building onto an upturned yoghurt or cream pot. This makes building No 4.

Cut two strips of card, 4 cm wide and 38 cm long, from a cereal packet. Place the two tops from the cheese boxes rim to rim and wrap a strip of card round the edges. Glue the strip in place to form a shallow drum shape, as shown.

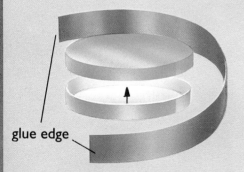

wrap strip around both boxes

glue edge

Now do the same with the two bottoms of the cheese boxes, again sticking the strip all the way around. Don't use a top and a bottom together as they are slightly different sizes and will not fit properly.

Using a pair of compasses, draw two circles, each with a diameter of 12 cm, on card. On each of them, draw a line from the edge to the centre point. Cut out the circles and cut along this line. Now overlap one edge over the other by 1.5 cm and stick these together, as shown, to form two very shallow cones. When these have stuck, glue them down onto a piece of card and when dry, cut around them. This forms a flat base to each cone.

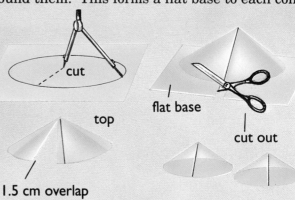

cut

flat base

top

cut out

1.5 cm overlap

8

Stick a bottle top, measuring approximately 2.5 cm high, onto the top of one of the drums made from the cheese boxes. Now stick two felt-tip pen tops either side of this near the edges, as shown. Stick the roof on top of these supports. Stick a yoghurt pot (Ski) to the bottom, as shown. Repeat this with the other drum and roof, so that you have two buildings the same.

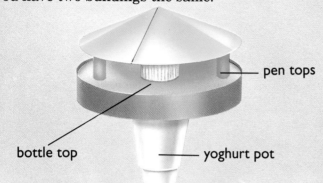

pen tops

bottle top — yoghurt pot

9

Cut eight strips of cereal packet card, 4 mm wide and 11 cm long. Bend these round into loops. Overlap the edges by 2 cm and glue them so that you have eight rings. Now stick these to the sides of the two buildings you have just made, as shown, four to each building. You now have buildings No 5 and 6.

side view

glue

top view

10

Stick the three soap boxes to the baseboard, as shown, and then glue the buildings in place. Glue two upturned bottle tops also in place, as shown, and then stick two ping-pong balls into these tops.

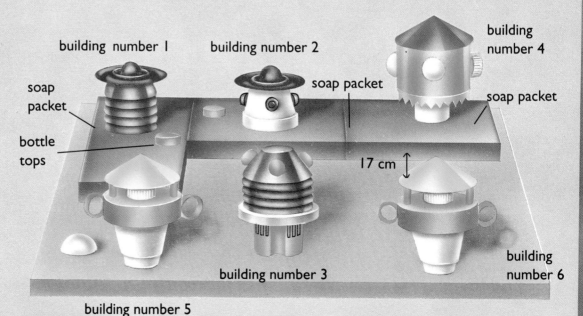

building number 1   building number 2   building number 4

soap packet   soap packet   soap packet

bottle tops

17 cm

building number 3   building number 5   building number 6

Titanica has a huge assortment of strange buildings, so you can add any other bottle tops or interesting shapes you want at this stage. Let your imagination really go!

You can now paint all the buildings in an assortment of colours, using the photo as a guide. They are generally silver but you can make them any colour you wish. When they are dry, mix a large packet of Polyfilla with water until you have a stiff paste, then mix in some brown powder paint. Using an old table knife and stiff paint

brush, model a rocky surface all over the baseboard, blending the soap boxes into the lower baseboard. While this is still wet, press pieces of lichen (obtainable from a model shop), or ordinary moss and other foliage into the Polyfilla to make a wonderful underwater landscape!

Finally, add pieces of clear tubing (obtainable very cheaply from a hardware or chemist's shop), to join the buildings together, as seen in the photo. You can stick these directly to the buildings or add supports made from plastic towel rail holders! This tubing is the underwater travel tube. Windows made from white sticky labels can also be added on buildings 5 and 6.

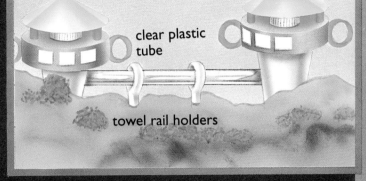

building number 5   building number 6

clear plastic tube

towel rail holders

Now beware Stingray because Titanica is waiting for you!

TITAN TERROR FISH

* 2 600 g cereal packets
* 2 ping-pong balls
* 2 tablespoons of Polyfilla
* UHU or Bostik glue
* Masking tape or sellotape
* Pair of compasses
* Scissors, craft knife
* Grey, brown, rust and white enamel paint

1

Use a pair of compasses to mark out a circle with a diameter of 20 cm on a piece of card. Cut out the circle and draw another circle with a diameter of 12 cm inside the first one. Draw lines to divide the outer circle up, as shown, and cut along these lines.

20 cm

12 cm

cut along the dotted lines

Next, cut a serrated edge, as shown, so that it looks like a cog wheel. These are the gills of the fish. Now draw a line from the outside edge to a point 2.5 cm from the centre. Cut along this line.

2

Draw one edge of the circle over the other to form an irregular cone, as shown. Glue the edges together and tape over, if necessary, to hold in place.

irregular cone

stick edges together

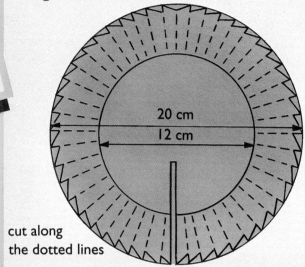

3

Mark out a semi-circle with a radius of 18 cm with compasses. Cut this out. Measure 18 cm from one corner to a point on the circumference. Draw a line to this point from the centre and cut this wedge off. Discard this piece.

cut

18 cm

4

Bend the rest of the semi-circle into the cone shape shown and tape the edges together.

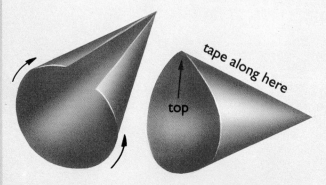

tape along here

top

This is the back of the fish's body.

Cut these shapes out of double thickness card.
(Stick the cereal packet card together with the grey sides out.)

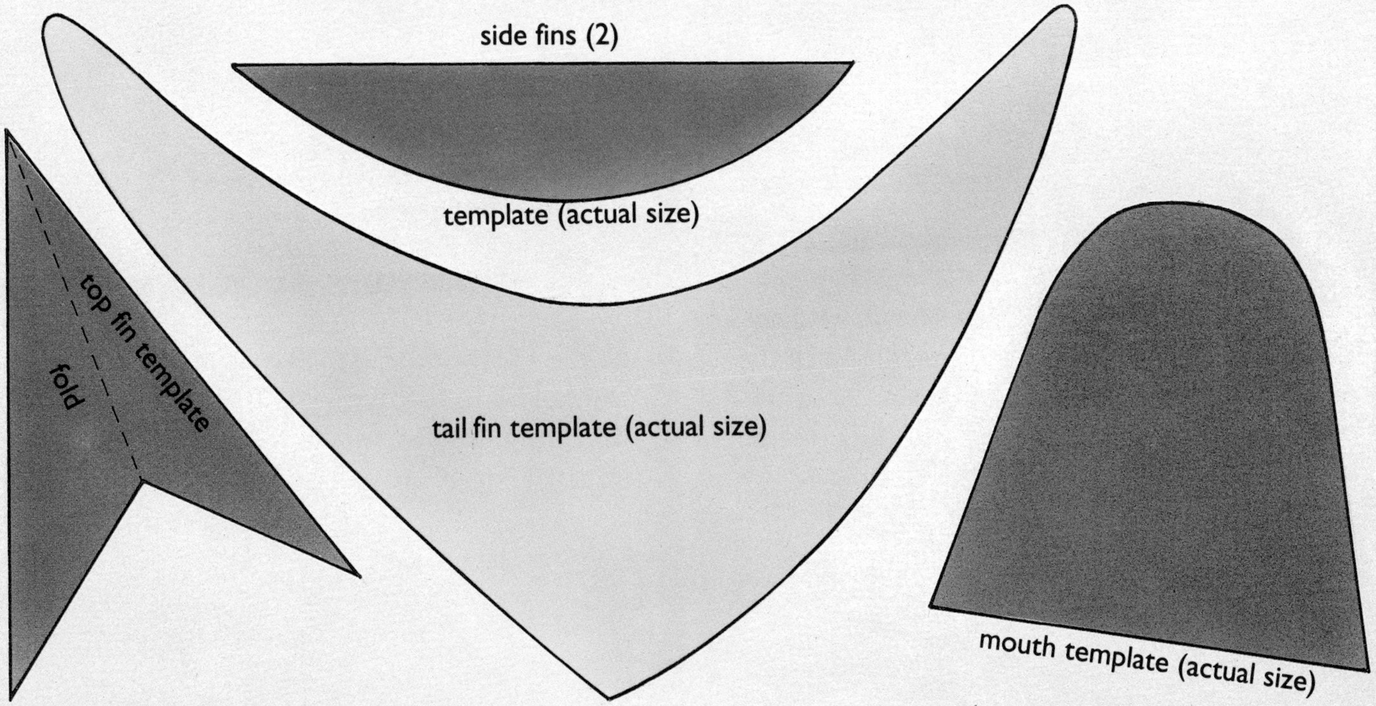

side fins (2)

template (actual size)

top fin template

fold

tail fin template (actual size)

mouth template (actual size)

Trace this head shape onto card and cut out.
Cut out the two circles shown.
These are where the eyes go.
Then, using a sharp knife, carefully
cut the two slots shown.

Bend the shape round
so that edges a and b
meet, and glue or
tape the edges
together.

You should now have
a shape like this.

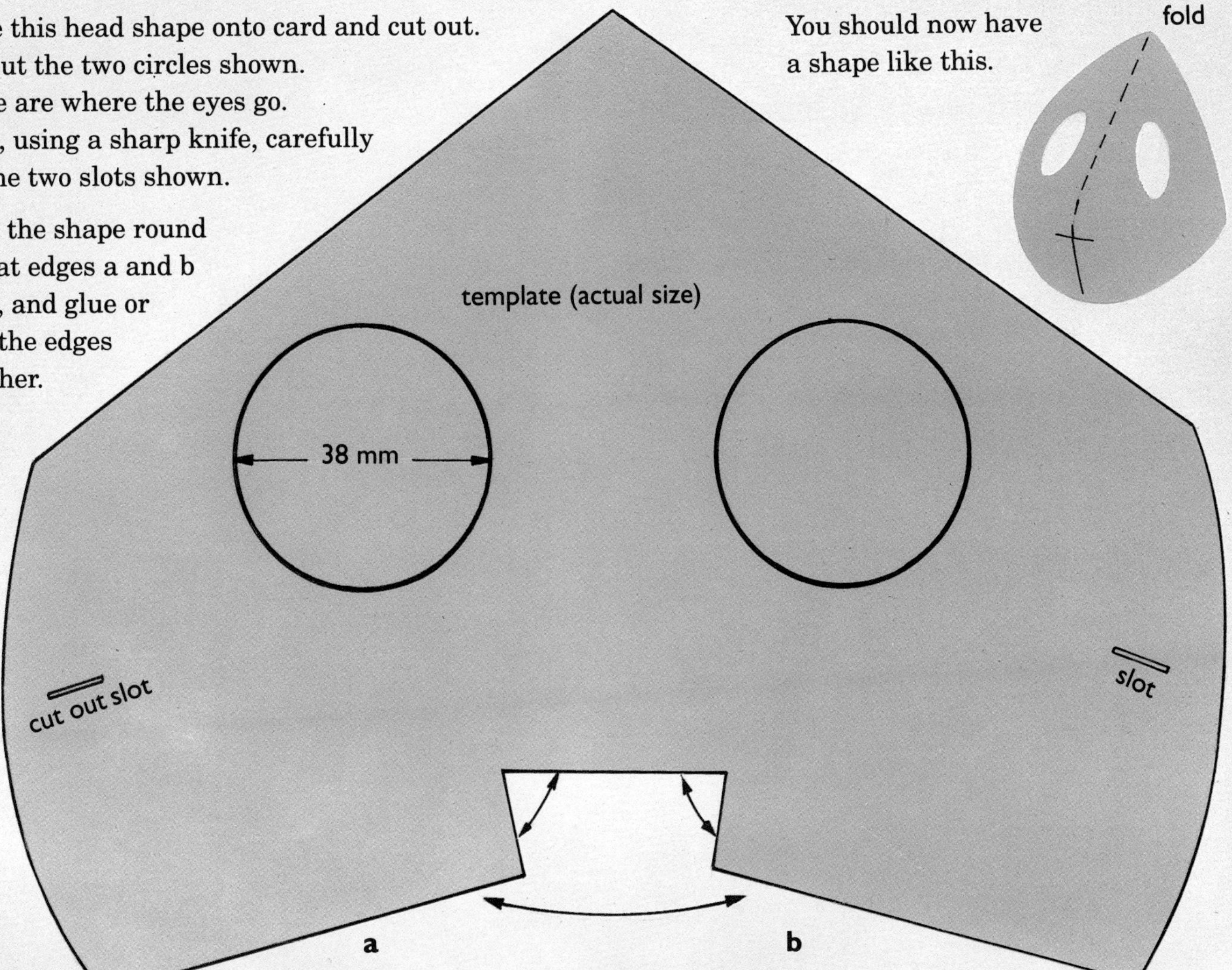

fold

template (actual size)

38 mm

cut out slot

slot

a   b

7

Cut two strips of double thickness cereal packet 13 cm long with one serrated edge, as shown. These are the fish's spines.

8

Cut two ping-pong balls in two just below the join line and throw away the bit with the writing on.

9

Glue all the pieces together, as shown, with the sharp edge of the long cone at the top. Stick the mouth flap so that it is slightly open. Allow to dry. Next, cut a 4 cm slot up the top and bottom of the back cone. This is for the tail fin.

10

Now stick the top fin in behind the gills and stick the tail fin in the rear slot. Then stick the side fins into the slots cut below the eyes so that the straight edges face forwards.

11

Mix two tablespoons of Polyfilla and some water into a thick creamy paste. Then, with a stiff bristle paintbrush stipple the front of the fish, as shown. Do not paint the eyes. Finally, paint the model using the photo as a guide.

You now have a Titan Terror Fish, the menace of the deep!

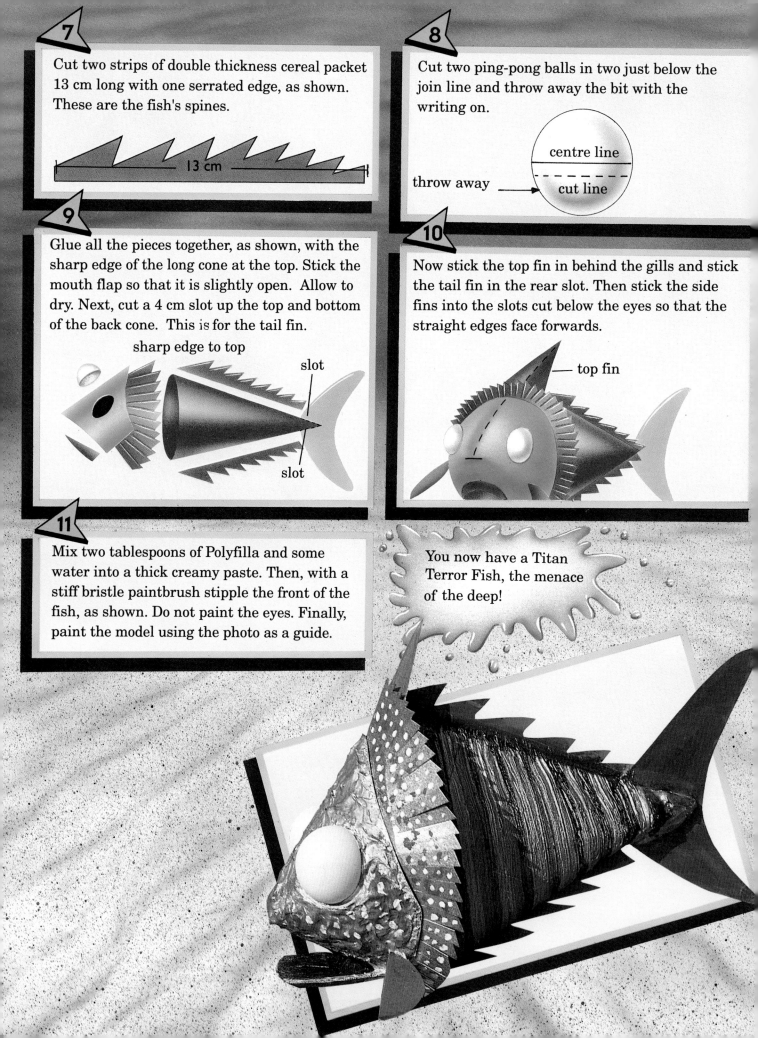

Cut out these logos and stick them on your Stingray models

Stingray

W.A.S.P Interceptor

SIDE HULL LETTERING

STINGRAY UNDERSIDE LETTERING

STINGRAY

TAIL FIN NUMBER

STRIPE FOR W.A.S.P. INTERCEPTOR

WASP

WASP

MISSILE SIDES

British Library Cataloguing in Publication Data

Bower, Martin
Make Your Own Stingray Models
I.Title II.
745.592

ISBN 0 340 60344 5

Impression 10 9 8 7 6 5 4 3 2 1
Year   1998 1997 1996 1995 1994 1993

The photograph of Titan, used on page 19 of this book, is used with the kind permission of David Finchett.

This book is supported by Fanderson, the official Gerry Anderson appreciation society. If you would like more information about Fanderson you can contact them at this address: Fanderson, PO Box 93, Wakefield, West Yorkshire, SR1 1XJ.

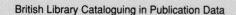